I HAVE TO LIVE WITH THEM?

UNDERSTANDING HOW BLACK AND BROWN CHRISTIANS NAVIGATE THEIR RELATIONSHIPS WITH WHITE CHRISTIANS IN THE AMERICAN CHURCH

I0190732

TERRELL CARTER

Energion Publications
Gonzalez, FL
2023

ISBN: 978-1-63199-856-0
eISBN: 978-1-63199-857-7

Energion Publications
P. O. Box 841
Gonzalez, FL 32560

energion.com
pubs@energion.com

DEDICATION

Someone once told me that there are no good writers, only good editors. Thanks, Zach Dawes for consistently helping me better communicate my thoughts and ideas about faith and race. It has been a pleasure to learn from you.

To Genevieve and Jerry Carter for life more abundantly.

INTRODUCTION — WHY DID I WRITE
ANOTHER BOOK ABOUT RACE?

Before you read this book, I want to share my story with you. I do this in the hope that you will better understand the point of view from which I write. I am a Black man raised by Black grandparents, Genevieve and Jerry, in a Black neighborhood. They were teenage parents who did not graduate from high school. My parents, Jerry and Vicky, were also teenage parents to me and my twin brother. Neither of them graduated from high school.

Our father was not an active part of our lives while we were growing up. When our mother was murdered when we were seven years old, our grandparents gained custody of us and raised us as their own. They raised us in love and the fear of the Lord. They modeled godly living for us, as well as encouraged us to believe in ourselves and to explore the creative gifts God had given us. For me, that meant making art. For my twin that meant creative writing.

In addition to being creative, I am a preacher-pastor. Technically I come from a line of them. I am a fifth-generation preacher-pastor. I answered my call to ministry when I was 16 years old and preached my first sermon when I was 17. After high school, my training for ministry occurred in historically white educational institutions: a conservative bible institute where I felt welcomed, a conservative seminary where I did not feel like my point of view or life experiences were understood or as valued primarily because they were so different from my professors and classmates, and a liberal seminary where my experiences were not only affirmed, but I was also encouraged to see God's presence in everyone I met.

I am a Black pastor who has primarily been called to serve within historically white contexts. The congregations where I have served as pastor were all at least 80% white when my service with them began. This is not a bad thing. They all had a history of welcoming diverse people, regardless of race, economic status, or anything else. During my service with these groups, I never felt anything but loved and respected by them.

In addition to the daily support of our grandparents, they also taught me and my twin that whatever we decided to do with our lives, or whatever God called us to do, we would have to be better at it than white people. They did not say this because they hated white people. They said it because they were raised in a generation that experienced the full brunt of Jim Crow segregation. Based on their experiences, two Black boys like us would not be treated well by the world. To have a fighting chance, we had to learn as much as we could and accept the opportunities that were available to us.

As adults, we have been afforded multiple opportunities to participate in new experiences due to our ability to code-switch. Code-switching has at least three linguistic purposes.

- The alternating or mixed use of two or more languages, especially within the same discourse.
- The use of one dialect, register, accent, or language variety over another, depending on social or cultural context, to project a specific identity.
- Modifying one's behavior, appearance, etc., to adapt to different sociocultural norms.[1]

We began to code-switch in high school, primarily to fit in. Code-switching is not necessarily a bad thing. This ability has served me well, both personally and professionally. Personally, it helped to open doors for me to form relationships with people who did not understand the Black experience or culture. Professionally, it helped me learn and speak the language of companies and institutions where I wanted to work. An irony of this ability to code-switch has been that my ability to speak like this has made me less appealing to traditional Black congregations whom I hoped to serve.

---

1 Code-switching. Dictionary.com. https://www.dictionary.com/browse/
code-switching?s=t. Accessed 2/16/21.

I have spent my professional and pastoral life serving others, regardless of ethnicity or income. For five years I served as a police officer for the city of St. Louis patrolling two of the most dangerous districts in the city. One district was primarily occupied by Black residents, while the other was made of a mixture of ethnicities. I served as executive director of two nonprofit organizations that served "urban poor," code for Black people. I have also taught at multiple colleges and universities.

I mention all these qualifications not as a way to brag, but to say they are integral to my journey to, in the words of my grandparents, give myself a fighting chance to be considered equal to white people and worthy of their trust and to gain access to the opportunities that come in being in relationship with them.

In addition to these qualifications, I have written 16 books that try to answer the question, "How can we help people build and strengthen their relationships with those who are different from them?" Four of these books explored the historic differences in how Black and white Christians have lived and been treated in the United States. In each of those books, I provided a list of recommendations for improving the historically divided relationships. This book is different from my prior ones in that I will not offer many solutions, instead, I will outline from a Black and Brown Christian perspective why these historic divides exist.

But rest assured, I am not writing from a position of anger. I am writing because I desire reconciliation for the relationships between Black, Brown, and white Christians in America. Reconciliation is a biblical concept. We typically think about it as something that primarily occurs between God and humankind due to our sin and how it separates us from our sinless God and our need to be reconciled to God. But reconciliation encompasses a lot more than the relationships between the Creator and the created. It includes the restoration of relationships between humans. We find an example of this in the book of Hosea.

The book of Hosea is primarily about two things: First, God has determined that there would be a day when God's children, both nations of Israel and Judah, would experience a reckoning due to their decisions to worship false gods instead of the one true God. Second, although there would be a reckoning, God still loved God's children and those children would one day be restored to full relationship with their Creator. Hosea prophesied to God's people before and during the reign of King Jeroboam, who became king of Israel after the southern kingdom of Judah and the northern kingdom of Israel separated. We are introduced to Jeroboam in 1 Kings 11:26.

In 1 Kings 11, a prophet told Jeroboam that God was taking the unified kingdom from Solomon and would give a portion to him. The reason that God was relieving Solomon of the unified kingdom was because Solomon worshiped false gods and entered military partnerships that went against God's wishes. Solomon's worship of false gods and placing his trust in foreign powers led to the king and the people turning their backs on God and trusting more in human abilities and partnerships.

Unfortunately, Jeroboam was no better than Solomon as a leader. Before his reign was complete, he had made most of the same mistakes as Solomon. So, God's people struggled to find adequate leadership and would eventually suffer the consequences of a lack of leadership. Enter Hosea, a nondescript preacher whose personal life was going to be an object lesson for God's people. The turbulence of God's relationship with God's unfaithful children was reflected in Hosea's turbulent marriage to an unfaithful woman named Gomer.

Hosea's prophecy began with God commanding him to marry this woman, to whom three children would be born as part of the relationship. The names of the children born during this time would reflect God's frustration with God's children and how God would respond to a nation that was not living into their covenant relationship. Eventually, Hosea's wife left their marital home and hooked up with a man that was not her husband. God commanded Hosea to go find her and bring her back home. Unbeknownst to Hosea, she was now a slave and he had to pay the cost to restore her. Hosea bought her freedom.

As you read the book of Hosea, multiple themes become apparent. There is the theme of forgiveness that Hosea and God show to their brides. There is the theme of staying true to your first love, whether that first love is God instead of other, false gods, or your spouse instead of other people. There is the theme that love, when given the opportunity, has the ability to restore relationships, no matter how damaged those relationships have become.

But there is another theme present that is as important as the two I mentioned. It is the theme of sowing and reaping. When someone sows negative things, they will reap negative things. When someone sows trust in false gods, they will reap the consequences that come with following false idols. When you sow trust in wrong relationships, you will reap the pain that comes when you find out that person did not truly care about you or have your best interest at heart. When you sow trust in everyone else but God, you will reap the consequences that occur when you see everyone else bow before God's might and authority. Every decision has consequences.

That is the point of this book. There are multiple examples throughout our nation's history of white Christians using the Bible and Christian faith as part of a process of worshiping false gods, especially as it relates to race. Those false gods have historically been the gods of power and position. When Black and Brown Christians have pushed back against these false gods by challenging the theologies that emphasize white preferences, desires, experiences, beliefs, and authority, our faith and fidelity to biblical principles have been questioned.

When we push back against what white Christians believe is the right thing to do, we are told that we are focusing on the wrong things. We are told that we should fix our own problems, first, before we try to address the inequities that have existed in our society. The point of this book is to use recent examples of what many white Christians believe to be faithful Christianity and why Black and Brown Christians do not view those examples as white Christians do. I write this book with the hope of bringing about restoration between groups who sometimes are at odds because we do not seem to be worshiping the same God.

Is Christian Nationalism the Answer or Part of the Problem?

Throughout America's history, we have witnessed multiple examples where Christianity has taken the shape that most benefits those who hold the greatest power to help them move their agendas forward. It is not hard to identify times when it has been used as a tool to force people to adapt and align with the stories and desires which Jesus would have stood against, such as the wholesale slaughter of indigenous Native Americans, the enslavement and torture of Africans and their descendants, the second-class status of women, and the marginalization of the poor, to name only a few historic sins.

Whoever has the political and social power to control the narratives being shared within our nation inevitably attempts to publicly shape the meanings of biblical stories and influence how our nation seeks to apply those stories to our context. The lessons these leaders usually share about the Bible and Christian faith have typically been that God wants what is best for our nation, even if the meaning of 'best' is defined by only a small group or if only a small percentage of people will receive the 'best' benefits.

The Bible's teachings about the gospel, which has historically meant the good news of God personally working for the common good of all creation to make salvation (both spiritual and physical restoration) available to all, has been replaced by a gospel of cultural and economic power and freedom that finds its center in the United States. This nationalistic theology naturally leads to questions about who will be allowed to experience the benefits of such a salvation.

I believe this nationalistic theology of "America first" is based not on a desire to be faithful to God's principles of large-scale restoration but is, in part, based on a fear of anyone who can be categorized as "other," whether due to skin color, gender identity, economic standing, or immigration status. Those who do not fit into clearly delineated boundaries set by the few in power are subject to rigorous critique to ensure they are worthy of experiencing the blessings inherent in American citizenship.

One of the ironies of this process of vetting the "other" is that those who do the vetting often fail to examine their own life circumstances. They hold the "other" to certain levels of moral responsibility that they do not follow themselves. They view them through the prism that if their lives have been covered in clouds of opportunity, personal and professional connections, and supportive educational and economic systems, the "other" should inherently know these opportunities are available to them, as well.

They forget that their lives may have been shaped by the benefits that come with being born into certain families or communities that "others" may not have had access to. Another challenge with this nationalistic theology is that it does not enable or encourage people to see the effects structural racism and classism and historic intentional inequalities have had on participants within our economic system. How can you, if you believe that everything a person has experienced in life is based on personal action or inaction?

Because we hold others to standards of life that we do not hold ourselves to, we fail to recognize the grace and fortune that we regularly experience in life, especially the grace found in being born within a specific timeframe and within family structures that may benefit us, and we fail to see "others" as God sees them. These practices, whether intentional or unintentional have helped to widen the gap between us and the people we consider unworthy of God's love or our compassion.

To more fully change our thinking about who does or does not hold value in our society, it will require us to re-imagine our relationship with the One who created all of us in the first place and how our relationships with God should influence how we view "others" and live in community together. We must remember that those in power are not the only people God loves or is concerned about. What we acquire in this world is not ours but has been given to us by God to bring salvation (both spiritual and physical restoration) to others.

God does not call us to first be successful in life, to gain property, to acquire possessions, or to align ourselves with political parties. God calls us to honor people over possessions and personal plans. When we fail to live into God's desires for us to treat others well and honor the gifts God has entrusted to us, like opportunities and possessions that could be used for the furtherance of God's kingdom, God's heart is broken and ultimately, God may call us to be accountable, as occurred in Hosea.

Like the prophets of old, during the times that we do become aware that we have fallen short of God's best for us, we should confess, repent, and fast (willingly sacrifice a certain level of our personal comfort) to show God that we are serious about living into the relationships God has called us to. We do this not for our own ego, to appease our conscious, or to make our nation great, but we do it to be formed into the people and nation God wants us to be for God's glory.

Although Donald Trump is no longer president, the continually divisive Conservative tropes and language that led to him being elected in the first place still hover like a cloud over our nation. These tropes and language are not new. His tactics derived from a movement called the Lost Cause of the Confederacy (the Lost Cause, for short) that was implemented by Southern sympathizers soon after the Civil War ended in 1865. Lost Cause sympathizers were not willing to accept the military, social or political defeat of their platform, one which was shaped by the idea that whites had an ordained right to own Black slaves. So, they sought to distort and revise the purpose behind their choice to stand against the Union while simultaneously reframing their intent as a glorious and God-ordained act that was honorable.

Beginning in 1866, the Lost Cause concept allowed the previous actions of Confederate leaders to be re-imagined through a lens of heroism by reinterpreting the purpose of the war and its subsequent fallout. Lost Cause advocates attempted to recast the genesis of the war from being about slavery instead to the idea of "state's rights." But what rights did the Southern states work so hard to keep? The right to maintain slavery. They also attempted to reframe their aggressive stand for slavery as an impassioned response to Northern attempts to dismantle the long-held Southern way of life.

Lost Cause proponents did this by reframing the myths, symbols, and rituals related to Southern life and the Confederacy. The myths they propagated were:

- That the South was a place primarily focused on nobility and chivalry and not on building an economy that was driven using Black bodies.
- That the enslavement of Black people was a noble cause because it provided these "savages" the opportunity to become Christianized.
- That white-dominated society was a primary part of God's intentions for the nation, as evidenced through the idea of manifest destiny.

The symbols they protected were the Confederate flag (which struck immediate fear in Black people), plantation life (which had as its foundation the unpaid and often severely punished service of Black bodies), and the Bible (which served as the ultimate source of power and control over those Black bodies). If a Black person was not willing to obey their masters as the Bible commanded, they had no hope for God's earthly protection or entrance into God's heavenly home.

The rituals prolonged by the Lost Cause were the active re-subjugation (re-incarceration) of Blacks under the guise that Blacks were not able to take care of themselves, were prone to criminality, therefore did not deserve their freedom, and that slavery was an inherent good for them. Another equally emphasized ritual was that not only should Blacks serve whites, but women should serve men, and the poor should serve the wealthy. When Reconstruction ended in 1877, Lost Cause proponents had effectively succeeded in initiating their plan to reframe their original intentions and adopt a position as victims to unrighteous Northern interference.

Unfortunately, this playbook has been updated for the 21st century. There are people who lead our nation and churches today who are attempting to hinder the full inclusion of people who they have deemed not to fit their image of what good Americans, or good Christians, look like. They seek to do so by:

- Reframing those who do good for the poor and outcast as anti-American communists or socialists.
- Holding on to racist symbols from the past and framing opposition to those symbols as heretical and standing against tradition (which in the Lost Cause is always more important than doing good).
- Using the Bible as a convenient tool even when what the Bible teaches stands in direct opposition to what is being done, such as demonizing those who come to America for a better life (Leviticus 19:34).
- Pitting people against each other through fear tactics and by framing one side as undeserving of God's full love.

The irony of this is that God does not call us to be good Americans. God calls us to be good followers of Jesus even when that means we find ourselves on the opposite side of political, social, and economic powers. Unfortunately, white evangelical Christians and politicians continue to follow this playbook.

Is the Church the Hope of America?

Is the Church the hope of the world? Most Christians would likely respond with an immediate and resounding, "Yes." When Martin Luther King, Jr. asked and answered this question for a sermon writing exercise while as a student at Crozer Theological Seminary in 1948, his answer was less than enthusiastic.

King began the brief sermon writing assignment by saying, "It is a common saying in religious circles that the church is the hope of the world. This question inevitably leads the objective mind to a bit of doubt. He immediately asks, 'how can the church be the hope of the world when it is the most reactionary institution in society.' In other words, the church is supposed to be the most radical opposer of the status quo in society, yet, in many instances, it is the greatest preserver of the status quo."[2]

Ouch!

My more conservative friends will likely ignore the spirit and challenge of King's words and instead focus on something unrelated to his intentions, like accusing King of being a liberal communist, or womanizer, as if those two potential traits negate any truth that may be found in his statements.

As I read King's words, I recognize the hyperbole of phrases such as "most reactionary institution in society" and "greatest preserver of the status quo". But King's use of hyperbole does not necessarily negate the underlying truth behind his words. There are several things for which the church in America will eventually have to give an account regarding how it has contributed to past and current spiritual, economic, and cultural conflicts experienced by our nation.

The Church may not explicitly tell our political leaders, like President Trump, or social extremists on either end of any given

---

2 King, Jr., Martin Luther. "Is the Church the Hope of the World."
The Martin Luther King, Jr. Papers Project. http://okra.stanford.edu/transcription/document_images/Vol06Scans/14Sept1948-15Feb1950Isthe ChurchtheHopeoftheWorld.pdf. Accessed 1/13/21.

spectrum, to behave badly on our behalf. However, congregants still affirm their actions by continuing to vote for them, advocate for their exercise of authority, and parrot their false narratives about the illegitimacy of our voting processes, their assertions about who is a "true" patriot, and their steady misapplication of the First and Second Amendments of the Constitution.

I believe the Church should be asked to give an account of this because according to a New York Times analysis of exit poll data, 76% of white evangelical Christians voted for Trump in 2020.[3] Mr. Trump also garnered the second-highest total for votes cast in a presidential election in history. The highest was for the man who beat him. This was a clear affirmation by white evangelicals that they supported his political and theological views of power and leadership. Yet, this criticism is not only directed towards white Christians.

Although only a handful of Black and Brown people were spotted participating in the insurrection that occurred at the capitol on January 6, 2021, it is not hard to find people of color who are fans of Trump's rhetoric. Multiple Black business leaders, rappers, athletes, and prominent pastors publicly threw their support behind his words. Overall, data shows that Trump's support within the Black community increased between 2016 and 2020.[4]

Please understand that I am not against Trump or any other person because they are Republicans, and I am not for anyone because they are Democrats. I am against any action that seeks to subvert Jesus' teachings from Matthew 25:31-46, which was about Jesus' desire for his followers to love others, provide for the poor, feed the hungry, protect the helpless, and care for the imprisoned. Instead of making that our focus, many U.S. Christians seem more interested in gaining and preserving power and influence.

---

3   National Exit Polls: How Different Groups Voted. Election Exit Polls 2020 - The New York Times (nytimes.com). Accessed 1/13/21.
4   Collins, Sean. "Trump made gains with Black voters in some states. Here's why." https://www.vox.com/2020/11/4/21537966/trump-black-voters-exit-polls. Accessed 1/13/21.

King said it this way in his assignment, "What has happened is this: the church, while flowing through the stream of history has picked up the evils of little tributaries, and these tributaries have been so powerful that they have been able to overwhelm the mainstream. In other words, the church has picked up a lot of historical vices. This is the tragedy of the church, for it has confused the vices of the church with the virtues of Christ."[5]

Please do not take my critique of the Church in the U.S. as an indication that I am against it. I am a member of the Church universal and within a local congregation. I have placed my trust in Jesus as my Savior. I believe that we learn about God and God's plans for restoration in the Bible. I am a fan of the Church and have spent the past 30 years trying to understand it and encourage it to live into its true calling found in Matthew 25.

I acknowledge that there are multiple things that the Church is doing well and getting right, but the things that we have not done so well, at times, loom so large as to overshadow the good we have done. Any critique that I may offer about the Church comes from not only a place of love, but from the hope that we, the Church, would consistently follow the example of the One whom we say we believe in.

January 6, 2021 should go down in history as a day of reckoning not simply for our current political leadership, but also for the Church in America. The things that need to be reckoned with by the nation and the Church were reflected in the flags that were waived by the insurgents as they overtook the capital building attempting to stop the certification of our recent presidential election. These flags read "Trump: Make America Great Again," the Confederate flag, and flags emblazoned with the words "Jesus 2020" and "Proud Christian American." Each represents something our nation and the Church in America has struggled with for several years: our uneasy acceptance and recognition of American patriotism as a cardinal virtue, the challenges inherent in our worship of a cult

5   King, Jr., Martin Luther. "Is the Church the Hope of the World?"

of personality (especially related to our political leaders), and the Church's acceptance of Christian nationalism.

Since Trump's ascension to the presidency, our nation has seen a steady increase in activity by militant nativist groups, such as the Proud Boys, who cover themselves and their actions in the American flag. Groups such as these state that their desire is to protect the history of America, restore it to its prior glory, and make America great, again. They do not agree with how our nation has become more diverse or how it seeks to cooperate with other nations to improve our world. They believe that these actions are unpatriotic and that our nation's first concern should be to keep America for Americans.

Although white evangelicalism has not gone to the extreme lengths that certain militant groups have, multiple leaders within the white evangelical church regularly use similar language. Instead of saying "America First," they say, "America is God's chosen nation." After Trump won the presidential election, evangelical leaders even went so far as to say his election was an act of God that would set America back on the right path spiritually. Instead of setting our nation on a proper spiritual path, our nation has experienced some of its darkest days.

The actions of the mob on January 6, which were akin to those of the Confederate Army led by General Jubal Early as they attempted to storm the capitol during the Civil War in July 1864, were rooted in a disfigured form of patriotism that is based on the fear that accompanies the loss of power and influence. Trump and many of his supporters regularly expressed this fear during Barack Obama's presidency through phrases like "This is no longer my America" and "The America I loved is gone." This language was regularly parroted in evangelical congregations by leaders such as Al Mohler, Franklin Graham, Jerry Falwell, Jr., and Robert Jeffress. These leaders regularly taught that Trump was God's chosen agent for change and if you did not follow Trump, you were not a biblical Christian.

15

Our nation, and the Church, also fell victim to the cult of personality. A cult of personality refers to how "a regime or a political figure uses media, lies, spectacles, speeches, patriotism, and even the arts and demonstrations for one to create the perfect image of a leader."[6] Trump, whose prior claim to fame was being a celebrity real estate developer and television personality, was elected in part based on his celebrity status, charismatic personality, brash words, and willingness to be politically incorrect. He was not elected on his experience or ability as a political leader. He was elected, in part, out of a fear that America had become too liberal and was straying from its Christian roots. What does this say about our values and what we desire in public leadership?

Ultimately, I think Trump's presidency and the actions of those who vehemently follow his rhetoric affirm the American Church's ongoing belief in Christian nationalism which "Draws its roots from 'Old Testament' parallels between America and Israel, who was commanded to maintain cultural and blood purity, often through war, conquest, and separatism."[7] Due to this blind adherence, the Church in America is at a point of reckoning about our beliefs related to power, God's desires for the entire world to be blessed and not just America, and whether we are willing to embrace the entirety of God's word and not just passages that espouse the evils of abortion or sexuality. Unfortunately, I think we have forgotten that God is not concerned simply about single-issue politics.

6 https://www.betterhelp.com/advice/personality/what-does-the-cult-of-personality-entail/
7 Andrew L Whitehead, Samuel L Perry, and Joseph O Baker. "Make America Christian Again: Christian Nationalism and Voting for Donald Trump in the 2016 Presidential Election", *Sociology of Religion*, Volume 79, Issue 2, Summer 2018, Pages 147–171.

Doesn't Talking About Race Only Keep Us Divided?

In many ways, the evangelical church continues to follow the Lost Cause playbook as it relates to the concerns voiced by minority communities. This was evidenced at the end of 2020 when the presidents of the six Southern Baptist Convention (SBC) seminaries released a joint statement dismissing critical race theory (CRT) as being incompatible with their understanding of the gospel and the 2000 Southern Baptist Convention Faith and Message. The importance of this move is found in the fact that the SBC is the largest and most influential protestant denomination in America.

CRT is an academic framework used to explain how social, legal, political, and economic systems have been used to help certain people groups in America make economic, political, and social progress while simultaneously hindering others. Their primary pushback against the theory is that Marxism is part of its foundation, thus making it atheistic. One of the ironies of this statement was that those leaders disregarded CRT due to its founders being influenced by Marxism while ignoring the fact that the SBC found its origin in the belief that slavery was sanctioned by the Bible, thus making it a viable option for Christians. Apparently, the SBC can be redeemed from its negative beginnings, but a philosophical theory cannot.

Aside from the irony of six white seminary presidents dismissing an academic theory that seeks to hold white leaders accountable when they make decisions related to their relationships with people of color without input from those people of color, the joint statement further brought the disconnect between white evangelical Christians and Christians of color into focus. For example, the statement said that CRT had become an issue in the larger world only in the past few years (2018-2020). Ironically, that timeframe coincides with a greater push for addressing the national concerns of people of color, especially those related to their relationships with law enforcement, lending institutions, etc.

Evangelical denominations, like the SBC, fail to recognize that their thoughts about theology and culture in many ways stand in direct opposition to the lived experiences of the people they say they want to be in relationship with. What I mean by this statement is that many people of color believe the social, legal, political, and economic systems that shaped and continue to prop up America have been used to keep them at a disadvantage. Most evangelicals do not believe in systemic anything. Instead, they believe that a person's life turns out the way it does due to personal decisions made over time. Each person is solely responsible for how their lives turn out.

The following are four additional general characteristics of 21st-century evangelical culture:

- Individualism- Evangelicalism emphasizes a 'personal relationship' with Jesus through intellectual faith. One of the challenges inherent in this is the idea that the outcomes a person experiences are the results of personal action.
- Anti-intellectualism - The assumption that critical thinking hinders the gospel message of personal salvation which can result in a tendency to simplify any argument down to aspects of a person's personal salvation rather than engaging in careful reflection to understand underlying issues more fully, such as historic classism and racism.
- Anti-structuralism - Evangelicals often emphasize personal accountability at the expense of understanding structural effects. This leads to thinking that whatever may be wrong in a person's life is due solely to personal responsibility and legal, institutional, or political patterns do not have any effect.
- Biblically-based economic freedom – Evangelicals typically believe that the Bible teaches personal responsibility as it

18

relates to economic circumstances. They believe that, based on what the Christian scriptures teach, individual actions carry the greatest influence on a person's economic status.

One of the problems with this mode of thinking is the tendency to over-spiritualize most life circumstances in such a way that, even when the Gospels clearly show Jesus challenging his followers to understand and combat the systems that fostered discrimination, those passages get spiritualized or overlooked. Instead of following Jesus' example of pushing back against the systems that separate people into hierarchies based on race and gender, some evangelicals condemn efforts, like CRT, that seek to point out how current political systems are very unchristian.

This line of thinking does not enable or encourage people to see the big pictures of structural racism, sexism, classism, other historic intentional inequalities, and the effects each has on participants within our society. How can you, if you believe that everything a person has experienced in life is based on personal action or inaction? I am not saying that this type of thinking makes evangelicals or the SBC seminary presidents bad. What I am saying is that it hinders them from understanding the experiences of people whose lives are vastly different from their own.

Unfortunately, understanding others does not seem to be one of the primary concerns of evangelicalism or the SBC. Instead, it seems like the concerns are for people to affirm a system that does not want to be challenged to think more critically about itself or those it says it wants to be in relationship with. The reader may be thinking that Black and Brown people are wrong in this assumption, especially after thinking about the public support that the Black Lives Matter Movement (BLM) received in the second half of 2020 after multiple Black males and females were killed at the hands of white police officers and citizens.

Shouldn't We Be Talking About the Gospel More and Race Less?

Since the public demonstrations first began to occur in 2020 in response to George Floyd's very graphic and public killing under the knee of a Minneapolis police officer, and the shooting of Breonna Taylor, I have been presented with a specific question several times. White Christians have asked me if I think relationships between Black and white Christians are getting better. My consistent answer has been that I hope this type of support consistently continues, but history has shown us that it likely will not.

Please understand that I do not say this in a sarcastic or negative way. At this point in my life, I am trying to be a realist. History has shown us a few general truths about white support of Black causes, especially those that involve police. In general, for white people to stand with Black people against questionable police or citizen actions, the Black person who serves as the lightning rod that led to the event that calls white people to action must typically have an impeccable personal history.

One of the most obvious examples of this was Michael Brown, who was killed in 2014 by a white police officer. Mr. Brown was a flawed teenager whose youthful actions were used to justify his death and why white people could not support the Black Lives Matter movement. Similarly, other Black people who were not perfect were raked over the coals for a host of past "sins" that had nothing to do with the police interactions that led to their lives ending or being forever changed. For example, being delinquent on child support payments (Walter Scott and Eric Garner) or having DUI arrests in their past (Rodney King).

One of the ironies of the events surrounding George Floyd's death and the eventual public response was that he was not the poster child for what a "good" Black person is or should be. Yet many white people have been kind to his memory instead of using his past as justification for his life being taken. Before someone points to the fact that Mr. Floyd's death was the action that sparked so much support from white people, we must acknowledge that this support for a Black man with a checkered past is the exception, not the rule.

I do not understand why Mr. Floyd served as the spark for this new sense of outrage by white people when multiple other Black people were killed before him, but I am thankful that more people are now involved. Also, in general, white support for Black causes may start out strong, but the longer the challenges last and the more inconvenient participation in those causes becomes, the less likely white citizens will stick with it. Anger over the killing of a Black or Brown person typically lasts if there is nothing else vying for the collective attention. When that other thing occurs, whether it be a natural disaster, pandemic, or sporting event, that something else becomes bigger and more important, until another Black or Brown life is lost, and the cycle starts over again.

Recent history has shown us that if white support does continue, their attention will eventually be drawn away from the original cause and turned to something wholly different. Since Mr. Floyd was killed, we have seen multiple examples of protests starting peacefully only to turn destructive due to the actions of people who were clearly involved only to cause trouble. Also, we have seen in multiple cities public movements that started as acts of support for Black and Brown lives eventually turned into something else that co-opted the original movement. This was evidenced in "autonomous zones" that sprung up in Seattle and Portland that had nothing to do with protecting life.

What does this say to Black and Brown people about the support they may receive in the future? When you do receive support in the future, you better work as quickly as possible to get your demands for equality met before people get tired or bored and turn their attention to the next cause or object vying for their attention. If not, you may find yourself standing on the front lines with severely diminished support.

This is one of the primary challenges that Black and Brown Christians who want to work with white Christians regularly face. Inconsistent support or support that is based on their ability to live up to the standards that white Christians place on minority communities. Black and Brown Christians are expected to encourage members from their communities to avoid actions and language that would cause white Christians to become uncomfortable because when white Christians become uncomfortable, they will likely break off talking about the things that are important to minorities and change the conversation to theological discussions about why racial discussions detract from the broader need to share the gospel with all people.

I say this because whenever I try to engage most of my conservative white friends about the Church's need to take the lead in participating in tangible efforts to bring about racial reconciliation, the most common response they give me is that we do not need to keep talking about race or social justice issues because those subjects only bring up old wounds and foster separation. Instead, they say, we need to talk more about the gospel because the gospel is what changes people.

Make no mistake, I believe in the gospel and recognize its importance to Christians and the world. I have wholeheartedly bought into the idea that, in Jesus, God has made it possible for humankind to be restored to their Creator and that there is an afterlife where we will be in a more complete relationship with God. I spend every Sunday affirming that before the congregation I serve as pastor. But I do not believe that Jesus' sacrifice was primarily about all believers one day leaving earth never to return. I understand the words and actions of Jesus while he walked this earth to be saying the opposite. The gospel is about this world and those within it being substantially changed in the here and now.

Although I believe the sincerity of my friends when they say they believe we need more of the gospel, I do not think the problem in our nation is a lack of knowing the gospel. Throughout the history of our nation, the name of God has regularly been invoked and the name of Jesus has been confessed as Lord. I think the problem with this line of thinking is that the gospel they purport to follow is an abstract idea that is primarily concerned with going to heaven instead of imitating the tangible actions of Jesus, which was his consistent message about the Kingdom of God. We focus too much attention on getting ready to leave this place and not enough attention on making it a better place for those who are here.

In framing the gospel as primarily being about leaving, we fail to acknowledge that Jesus consistently talked more about his mission to serve people than to prepare people for a far-off place. Jesus taught more about performing acts of kindness for women, orphans, the poor, the oppressed, and the "other" than he did about traveling to heaven. Jesus did not teach much about leaving and instead taught his disciples how to change the world they occupied for God's glory and the benefit of others.

Jesus' gospel message was that God's kingdom was at hand. For Jesus, the Kingdom of God meant that the process of God's desire to be in true relationship with humankind was coming to fruition. And because it was appearing before their eyes, it should cause them to have better relationships with other people.

I must be truthful and say that I am less concerned about going away to heaven when I die, and I am more concerned about how this message should make a difference in the here and now in how people are treated and Jesus' attitude and acts of love for others can be imitated. The Church's failure to help make a difference in the ongoing conversations about race and reconciliation, or police—community challenges, or any of the other things that usually get brushed aside is partly due to a failure to understand what the gospel is truly about. It is not first about escaping to a faraway place of safety in God's arms. It is about God's act, through Jesus, of facing the uncomfortable sin that is human nature to bring reconciliation and healing to others in tangible ways.

Having confidence that one is going to heaven does not stop a person from being racist, sexist, classist, or any other "IST" we can think of. In many ways, primarily focusing on the future seems to encourage Christians to ignore the current needs and plight of certain people groups in favor of personal safety and comfort. I do not think this is the kind of gospel Jesus was trying to get his followers to live into.

WHAT DO WE DO WHEN WE FIND OUT WE MAY BE PART OF THE PROBLEM?

What do you think of when you hear the phrase "American Dream"? It usually means that if a person works hard and keeps their nose clean, they will achieve anything they want. Much of the nation's history, and the theology that has arisen from the church in America, stems from this belief. An often-unspoken reality of this dream is that it has not always been available to everyone in the U.S. For various ethnic minorities who came to America willingly or unwillingly, for women who were treated as second-class citizens, and for other groups, the American Dream has not always been something good or attainable.

This realization has caused me to ask, "What if a person's life is not as good as it could be due to how my personal desires and actions affect them?" An example of this question in action is found in the life of King Solomon who started out as a good and godly ruler, but his aspirations for grandeur began to negatively affect the people he ruled. In 1 Kings 5:13-16 and 1 Kings 9:15-23 we read that over a 20-year span Solomon forced various people groups to participate in multiple building projects that seemed to occur for the specific purpose of adding to his reputation and stature as king.

The first was the temple, which took seven years to build, then the king's palace, which was almost as huge and as palatial as the temple. Rebuilding several cities that had previously been destroyed during military conflicts under King David would follow. Aside from the plans that God gave Solomon's father, King David, for the building of the temple, it seemed everything else Solomon built was based on what he thought would improve Israel's standing among other nations and lead to potential partnerships with other nations that would benefit his kingdom.

This was reflected in how the Queen of Sheba responded when she visited him. She was thoroughly impressed with not only Solomon's wisdom but also with the physical stature of his construction projects. History tells us that other leaders were even more impressed with the construction of his throne, which apparently was the first of its kind to move via a pulley system.

While these actions do not negate the good that Solomon did in God's name and for his nation, they do shed light on the fact that Solomon used people who did not necessarily want to be involved to build his kingdom. Even in doing the Lord's work and trying to improve the standing of Israel, Solomon made choices that negatively affected people that had not done anything to him. In the end, it was decisions like these that led to a divided kingdom and people actively plotting to overthrow him.

When I think about the American Dream, I cannot help but remember that, among other things, our nation was formed in protest of this type of leadership and these types of forced labor practices. This brings us back to my original question: What should I do when I realize that I am the person making someone else's life hard? Is the appropriate response to ignore their pain and continue to live into "my right" to experience life, liberty, and the pursuit of happiness?

If I understand God's desires for how I should fashion my life according to Jesus' example, then the so-called American Dream should not be my first concern. Being a successful American does not equate to being a good Christian. Being a good Christian requires that I see beyond myself and the hopes of my nation or political tribe. That is what Jesus meant when he insisted that we love God and love others as ourselves.

In loving others as we love ourselves, we begin to understand that we do not only travel through life with people who are like us and are from our tribe. Instead, God invites us to be in relationship with people who are different from us and those we feel most comfortable with. In setting our comfort aside, we get a glimpse of what God's future kingdom will look like.

CONCLUSION

At the beginning of this book, I mentioned Hosea. One of the themes of Hosea is accountability. Corporate and personal accountability for choices made and the spiritual, political, and communal reckoning that follows. As the people in Hosea had the opportunity to understand how their personal and corporate choices affected every aspect of their lives, but most importantly their relationships with God and each other, America has the same opportunity.

In general, Black and Brown people love America and recognize the blessings that come from being here. But, we do not love how we have historically been treated as America has sought to become the greatest nation. Black and Brown Christians also love our white brothers and sisters, but we do not love how our lived experiences or points of view are relegated to the back of the theological bus. We earnestly seek reconciliation with our white brothers and sisters, but that restoration does not begin with our conformity to white expectations that minimize our experiences, beliefs, or feelings. It does not begin with portraying our experiences, beliefs, or feelings as anti-gospel because they may cause some white people to feel uncomfortable.

Our nation is primed to experience the types of turbulent times that Hosea predicted. Many in our nation prefer to follow the false idols of commerce and commercialism than to follow God's command to do justice, love mercy, and walk humbly with our Creator through the relationships we have with others here on earth. We worship the false idols of nationalism and patriotism instead of following God's commandment to love the least of these. There are consequences to this. The consequences are that these idols will be smashed and ground down and God will require human accountability.

A question we all must answer is "Who among us is willing to be God's agent to call our nation to accountability?" God wants followers who are willing to call God's people to a life of faithfulness

27

during a time when people are more concerned about themselves and their economic or political futures. God reminds us that there are consequences when we put prestige, politics, and money first over faithfully living out our relationship with our Creator and the rest of creation.

Recognizing the part that you play in this story can serve as the launching point for becoming prepared and equipped to call people to stand on God's side and to learn to lead during turbulent times as the prophets of old did. A way to show that you are willing to live into this holy call for human reconciliation is to embrace the opportunities to learn from people who are different from you. As I have shown in the prior pages, one of the primary challenges our nation faces today is how we can interact in meaningful ways with people who are different from us or how to develop relationships with them. This is true even for Christians.

There are multiple reasons for this challenge. Some of the reasons revolve around theological, political, and social tribalism that leads to an unintentional disconnect between what we understand the Bible to say about relationships and what our tribes, those who believe the same thing we do and those who do not, tell us about who we can and cannot have beneficial relationships with. The relationship between different people groups and, subsequently, how they should treat each other, is important to God—so much so that relationships between tribes are addressed in multiple places in the Bible.

In the Hebrew Bible, God told the children of Israel that when they finally entered the Promised Land, the land that symbolized God's faithfulness to fulfill generations-old promises to take care of them and provide for them in new ways, they were to remember that they had once been slaves and wanderers in a strange land who did not always have enough. Remembering this chapter of their lives should have caused them to have compassion towards other tribes with whom they interacted.

For example, in honor of God's faithfulness in providing for the children of Israel, they were not to hoard all the fruit which the land produced for themselves. Instead, they were to forgo reaping every piece of fruit and grain and leave some of the excess the land produced to be reaped by the poor and hungry from their own tribes, as well as from other nations, to use for their own needs. The new land was not only for their self-preservation but for the preservation of multiple people groups.

Unfortunately, I think we have forgotten that God does not care primarily about the political desires of one group over another. God cares more about how we view and treat each other and how we reflect God's presence before others. God also cares about how our actions affect others around us.

In his *Letter from Birmingham City Jail*, Dr. Martin Luther King, Jr. talked about the reason we should have a larger view of life and how we interact with people who are different from us or our preferred tribe. Dr. King wrote, "We are caught in an inescapable network of mutuality, tied in a single garment of destiny. Whatever affects one directly, affects all indirectly."[8]

Mutuality and destiny are often ignored biblical principles. Mutuality in the sense that we should hold each other in high esteem and treat others with respect because we each were created in God's image. Destiny in the sense that we do not inhabit this world or life by ourselves. We do so in conjunction with the journeys of others. Not only do we travel through this life together, but we will also experience the same process of accountability for how we treated each other when we encounter God in the afterlife.

Will embracing the ideas of mutuality and common destiny fix all the ills that plague our nation? No, they will not, but adopting those principles can be the first step in the process to heal our nation and begin to make America great again.

---

8 King, Jr., Martin Luther. "Justice." National Civil Rights Museum. https:// mlk50.civilrightsmuseum.org/justice. Accessed 3/16/21.

Topical Line Drives

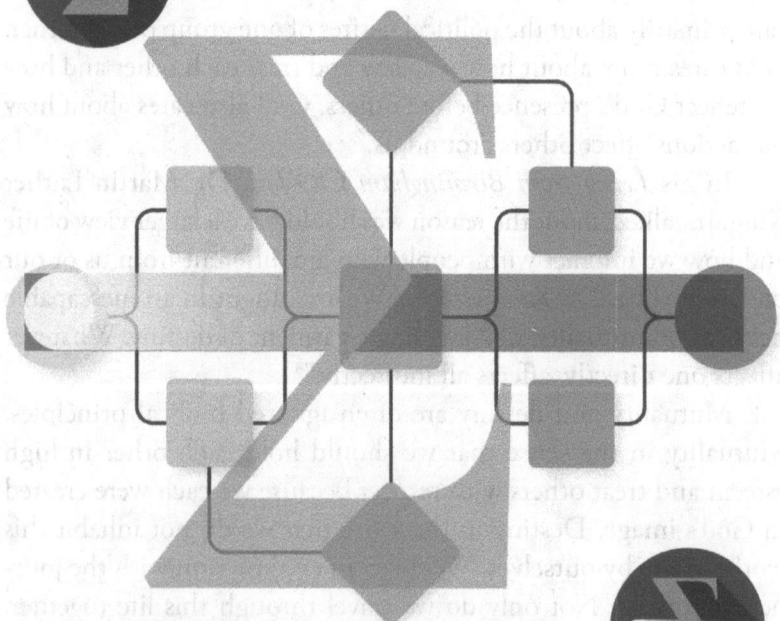

www.ingramcontent.com/pod-product-compliance
Lightning Source LLC
Chambersburg PA
CBHW011750020426
42331CB00014B/3347